Diabetic Dessert Cookbook

Delicious And Healthy Diabetic Dessert Recipes

Table of Contents

Introduction

Chapter 1: Diabetic Pie And Cake Recipes

Chocolate Espresso Cake

Zesty Lemon Cheesecake

Chocolate Sponge Cake

Apple Cinnamon Cake

Chocolate Apple Cake

Walnut Apple Cake

Apple Pie

Cranberry Pound Cake

Chocolate Fudge Nut Cake

Crustless Pumpkin Pie

Applesauce Raisin Cake

Easy Peanut Butter Squares

Chapter 2: Diabetic Cookie And Brownie Recipes

Chocolate Walnut Brownies

Banana Peanut Butter Cookies

Pumpkin Cinnamon Cookies

Almond Cookies

Gingersnap Cookies

Honey Raisin Cookies

No-Bake Oatmeal Coconut Cookies

Peanut Butter Cookies

Banana Oat Cookies

Banana Cookies

Raisin Oatmeal Cookies

Chocolate Chip Cookies

Cheesecake Brownies

Banana Oatmeal Raisin Cookies

Butterscotch Cookies

No Bake Oatmeal Peanut Butter Cookies

Introduction

Diabetes can be a serious and debilitating condition. For those suffering from this disease, the right diet is extremely important. Consuming a diet rich in vegetables and fruits is vital for controlling diabetes, and avoiding certain foods that can make diabetes worse is just as important. One of the main causes of diabetes is consuming a poor diet that contains high amounts calories, sodium and sugars.

Here are some helpful dieting tips for controlling diabetes:

- Consume healthy carbs, these contain a lower glycemic index and will make you feel full for longer. Healthy carbs include whole grains, fruits, nuts, beans.

- Include fresh seafood in your diet. Salmon, cod and tuna are low in fat and some fish like salmon are natural sources of omega-3 fats.

- Consume meals that are well balanced. Proper meals should be at least half vegetables, and only ¼ of your meal should include meat!

This cookbook contains a healthy collection of recipes that are diabetic friendly. These recipes will keep you on the right track for controlling this disease and living a healthy lifestyle. Many people assume that once one has diabetes, then they must be on a strict diet that is boring and painful to keep this disease in check. This is clearly false, the recipes in this book are just as delicious as any other non-diabetic recipes!

Chapter 1: Diabetic Pie And Cake Recipes

Chocolate Espresso Cake

Ingredients

1 ⅔ cups flour

3/4 cup Splenda + 1/4 cup brown Splenda

⅔ cup unsweetened baking cocoa, sifted

1 ½ teaspoons baking soda

1 teaspoon salt

½ cup applesauce

1 ½ cups skim milk low fat yogurt

1 tablespoon vanilla

1 tablespoon instant coffee

3 egg whites

1 egg yolk

Directions

Set oven to 350°F.

Generously grease a 13 x 9-inch baking pan.

In a medium bowl sift the flour with cocoa powder, instant coffee, baking soda and salt.

In another bowl beat the Splenda with eggs and vanilla until well combined. Mix in the yogurt and applesauce until thoroughly combined.

Mix the wet ingredients into the dry ingredients and beat on low speed until just combined. Transfer to prepared baking dish.

Bake for about 30-35 minutes or until cake appears done.

Nutrition: 126 Calories; 1g fat; 27g Carbohydrates; 4g Protein; per 1/18 of recipe

Zesty Lemon Cheesecake

Ingredients

2 tablespoons cold water

1 envelope unflavored gelatin

2 tablespoons lemon juice

1/2 cup skim milk, heated almost to boiling

Egg substitute equivalent to 1 egg, or 2 egg whites

1/4 cup sugar

1 teaspoon vanilla

2 cups low-fat cottage cheese

Lemon zest

Directions

Combine water, gelatin and lemon juice in blender container. Process on low speed 1 to 2 minutes to soften gelatin.

Add hot milk, processing until gelatin is dissolved. Add egg substitute, sugar, vanilla and cheese to blender container. Process on high speed until smooth.

Pour into 9-inch pie plate or round flat dish. Refrigerate 2 to 3 hours. If you wish, top with grated lemon zest just before serving.

Nutrition: 80 Calories; 9g Carbohydrates; 1g Fat; 9g Protein; per 1/8 of recipe

Chocolate Sponge Cake

Ingredients

4 egg whites

¼ teaspoon cream of tartar

¼ teaspoon salt

⅓ cup sugar

2 egg yolks

1 teaspoon vanilla

¼ cup all-purpose flour

¼ cup cocoa

Directions

Line an 8 inch square or round cake pan with waxed paper.

Place egg whites, cream of tartar and salt in a mixing bowl, beat with electric mixer until foamy.

Beat in sugar gradually, continue beating until stiff peaks form. Beat in egg yolks and vanilla.

Combine flour and cocoa and fold lightly into egg mixture. Spread batter in prepared pan.

Bake in 325F degree oven 25-30 minutes or until cake springs back when lightly touched. Loosen sides with a sharp knife.

Turn out immediately onto a paper towel lined cake rack to cool.

Nutrition: 52 Calories; 1g fat; 9g Carbohydrates; 2g Protein; per 1/12 of recipe

Apple Cinnamon Cake

Ingredients

⅔ cup flour

½ cup whole wheat flour

1 teaspoon baking soda

1 teaspoon cinnamon

¼ teaspoon salt

1 ½ cups peeled cored and finely chopped apples

¼ cup fat-free liquid egg product

1/2 cup Splenda + 1/4 cup brown sugar

½ cup chopped walnuts or ½ cup pecans

¼ cup applesauce

1 tablespoon flour

1 tablespoon whole wheat flour

½ teaspoon cinnamon

1 tablespoon butter

¼ cup walnuts or ¼ cup pecans

Directions

Lightly coat a 9-inch baking pan with cooking spray; set aside.

In a medium bowl combine the 2/3 cup flour, 1/2 cup whole flour, soda, 1 teaspoon cinnamon, and salt, set aside.

In a large mixing bowl toss together the chopped apple and egg product; stir in the 3/4 cup sugar, the 1/4 cup nuts and applesauce. Add flour mixture and stir until just combined.

Pour batter into prepared pan.

To Make Topping:

Stir together the brown sugar the remaining flour, whole wheat flour and cinnamon; Cut in butter until crumbly, stir in remaining nuts, sprinkle topping over batter in pan.

Bake in 350F oven 30 to 35 minutes or until a toothpick comes out clean; cool in pan for 10 minutes, serve warm.

Nutrition: 217 Calories; 7g fat; 37g Carbohydrates; 3g Protein; per 1/10 of recipe

Chocolate Apple Cake

Ingredients

¾ cup whole wheat flour

¾ cup flour

1 teaspoon baking soda

¼ cup cocoa

½ teaspoon salt

1 cup water

¼ cup applesauce

1 teaspoon lemon juice

1 teaspoon vanilla

1 apple, chopped and peeled (1 cup)

3/4 cup Splenda

½ teaspoon cinnamon

Directions

Oven to 350F°.

Spray a square pan with nonstick spray, I used a glass pan. Combine first 5 ingredients in bowl.

In another bowl, combine water, oil, lemon juice, vanilla. Add to dry ingredients, stir until just combined.

Toss apples with sugar and cinnamon, fold into batter. Pour into prepared pan.

Bake for 30-35 minutes or until done.

Nutrition: 141 Calories; 1g fat; 32g Carbohydrates; 3g Protein; per 1/9 of recipe

Walnut Apple Cake

Ingredients

1 ½ cups low-fat buttermilk

1 cup organic rolled oats

½ cup applesauce

2 beaten eggs (or 1/2 cup Eggbeaters)

¼ cup honey or ¼ cup Splenda granular

1 cup whole wheat flour

½ cup unbleached self raising flour

1 ¼ teaspoons baking powder

¾ teaspoon ground cinnamon (or to taste)

¼ cup roughly chopped walnuts

2 tablespoons sultanas

Directions

Combine the buttermilk and rolled oats in a bowl and set aside for 15-20 minutes until the oats have softened.

While the buttermilk and oats are standing, pre-heat your oven to 350°f and line a standard baking tin with greaseproof paper.

Beat the eggs and add to the oatmeal mix along with the applesauce.

If using honey add to wet ingredients. It using Splenda add to dry ingredients.

Mix the dry ingredients together, stirring to combine and add to the wet, mixing well.

Transfer the solid batter into the prepared baking tin. Using a wooden spoon, spread the batter to even it out.

Sprinkle the cake with roughly chopped walnuts and sultanas and let it sit for 20 minutes before baking.

Bake cake for approximately 1 hour or until a skewer inserted into the cake comes out clean.

Nutrition: 141 Calories; 1g fat; 32g Carbohydrates; 3g Protein; per 1/9 of recipe

Apple Pie

Ingredients

1 cup dry rolled oats

1/4 cup whole-wheat pastry flour

1/4 cup ground almonds

2 tablespoons brown sugar, packed

3 tablespoons canola oil

1 tablespoon water

Filling

6 cups sliced and peeled tart apples (about 4 large apples)

1/3 cup frozen apple juice concentrate

2 tablespoons quick-cooking tapioca

1 teaspoon cinnamon

Directions

To prepare pie crust, mix dry ingredients together in a large mixing bowl. In a separate bowl, mix oil and water together with whisk. Add oil and water mixture to dry ingredients. Mix until dough holds together.

17

Add a bit more water if needed. Press dough into a 9-inch pie plate. Set aside until filling is prepared.

To prepare filling, combine all ingredients in a large bowl. Let stand for 15 minutes. Stir and then spoon into prepared pie crust.

Bake at 425 F for 15 minutes. Reduce heat to 350 F and bake 40 minutes, or until apples are tender.

Nutrition: 204 calories; 8 g fat; 29 g carbohydrates; 4 g protein; per cookie

Cranberry Pound Cake

Ingredients

2 cups all-purpose flour

1 ¼ teaspoons baking powder

½ teaspoon baking soda

3 tablespoons butter, softened

½ cup Splenda Sugar Blend for Baking

2 eggs

¼ teaspoon orange extract (optional)

⅔ cup plain nonfat yogurt

2 cups fresh cranberries

¼ cup water or ¼ cup orange juice

1 ½ teaspoons orange zest, finely grated

Directions

Preheat oven to 350F. Prepare bundt or tube pan with a light coat of cooking spray.

In a medium bowl, sift together the flour, baking soda and baking powder.

In a large bowl, cream the butter with an electric mixer. Add Splenda blend and beat until pale, light and fluffy. Add the eggs, one at a time, mixing after each addition for a total of two or three minutes. If want more orange flavor, mix in the orange extract at this step.

Mix together the yogurt and water or orange juice.

Add in the cranberries, folding in to distribute throughout the batter.

Pour batter into the prepare tube pan and bake for 40 minutes or until an inserted toothpick comes out clean.

Cool cake in pan for 10 minutes until turning onto cake rack or plate.

Nutrition: 161 Calories; 4g fat; 27g Carbohydrates; 4g Protein; per 1/12 of recipe

Chocolate Fudge Nut Cake

Ingredients

½ cup whole-wheat pastry flour

½ cup all-purpose flour

⅓ cup sugar or 3 tablespoons Splenda Sugar Blend for Baking

¼ cup unsweetened cocoa powder, sifted

1½ teaspoons baking powder

½ teaspoon salt

1 large egg

½ cup 1% milk

2 tablespoons canola oil

2 teaspoons vanilla extract

¾ cup semisweet chocolate chips

1⅓ cups hot brewed coffee

⅔ cup packed light brown sugar, or Splenda Granular

¼ cup chopped walnuts, or pecans, toasted

Confectioners' sugar, for dusting

Directions

Preheat oven to 350°F. Coat a 1½- to 2-quart baking dish with cooking spray. Whisk whole-wheat flour, all-purpose flour, sugar or Splenda Sugar Blend, cocoa, baking powder and salt in a large bowl.

Whisk egg, milk, oil and vanilla in a glass measuring cup. Add to the flour mixture; stir with a rubber spatula until just combined.

Fold in chocolate chips, if using. Scrape the batter into the prepared baking dish. Mix hot coffee and brown sugar or Splenda Granular in the measuring cup and pour over the batter.

Sprinkle with nuts.

Bake the pudding cake until the top springs back when touched lightly, 30 to 35 minutes. Let cool for at least 10 minutes. Dust with confectioners' sugar and serve hot or warm.

Nutrition: 162 Calories; 22g Carbohydrates; 7g Fat; 4g Protein; per 1/8 of recipe

Crustless Pumpkin Pie

Ingredients

1 (15 ounce) can pumpkin puree

1/2 cup skim milk

1 (1 ounce) package instant sugar-free vanilla pudding mix

1 teaspoon pumpkin pie spice

1 (8 ounce) container fat free frozen whipped topping

Directions

In a medium bowl, mix together the pumpkin, milk, and instant pudding mix. Stir in the pumpkin pie spice, and fold in half of the whipped topping.

Pour into an 8-inch pie plate, and spread remaining whipped topping over the top. Chill for 1 hour, or until set.

Nutrition: 110 Calories; 0g fat; 23g Carbohydrates; 1.5g Protein; per 1/6 of recipe

Applesauce Raisin Cake

Ingredients

2 cups all-purpose flour

1 teaspoon baking powder

1 teaspoon baking soda

1/2 teaspoon ground cinnamon

1/2 teaspoon ground nutmeg

1/2 teaspoon salt

1 1/2 cups unsweetened applesauce

3/4 cup brown sugar twin

2 eggs

1 teaspoon vanilla extract

1/2 cup raisins

Directions

Preheat oven to 350 degrees F (175 degrees C). Spray an 8x4 inch loaf pan with cooking spray.

Sift together flour, baking powder, baking soda, cinnamon, nutmeg and salt. Set aside.

Beat the eggs until light and add sugar twin. Add applesauce and vanilla.

Add flour mixture and beat until smooth. Fold in raisins.

Pour batter into loaf pan. Bake at 350 F (175 degrees C) for about an hour, or until a toothpick inserted into cake comes out clean.

Nutrition: 125 Calories; 1g fat; 26g Carbohydrates; 3g Protein; per 1/12 of recipe

Easy Peanut Butter Squares

Ingredients

1 box butterscotch pudding jello (sugar and fat free mix)

6 1 oz squares baker's white chocolate

1/2 cup peanut butter (smooth, with salt)

3 cups Stevia (Powdered measures like sugar)

1/4 cup mixed nuts, dry roasted, chopped

1/3 cup water

Directions

Line an 8" square pan with foil, leaving ends sticking out to use as handles later.

In a microwave bowl combine 6 oz white Bakers chocolate, 1/2 cup peanut butter and 1/3 cup water. Cook on high 1 1/2 minutes and stir, repeat until smooth.

Add dry pudding mix, whisk 2 minutes. Gradually stir in Stevia. Spread in the bottom of 8" square pan. Top with chopped nuts, pressing down to secure.

Refrigerate 2 hours, lift from foil edges and flip onto cutting board.

Nutrition: 93 calories; 6 g fat; 7 g carbohydrates; 2 g protein; per 1/24 of recipe

Chapter 2: Diabetic Cookie And Brownie Recipes

Chocolate Walnut Brownies

Ingredients

1/2 cup margarine

1/4 cup unsweetened cocoa powder

2 eggs

1 cup granular sucrolose sweetener

1/4 teaspoon baking powder

1/2 teaspoon vanilla

3/4 cup all-purpose flour

1/8 teaspoon salt

1/4 cup 2% milk

1/2 cup chopped walnuts

Directions

Preheat oven to 350 degrees F (175 degrees C). Grease and flour an 8x8 inch pan.

In a small saucepan over medium heat, melt margarine and cocoa together, stirring occasionally until smooth. Remove from heat and set aside to cool. In a large bowl, beat eggs until frothy. Stir in the sucrolose sweetener. Combine the flour, baking powder and salt; stir into the egg mixture then mix in the vanilla, cocoa and margarine.

Finally stir in the 1/4 cup of milk and the walnuts. Pour into the prepared pan.

Bake for 25 to 30 minutes in the preheated oven, until a toothpick inserted into the center, comes out clean.

Nutrition: 129 calories; 4g fat; 24g carbohydrates; 2g protein; per 1/12 of recipe

Banana Peanut Butter Cookies

Ingredients

1 ½ cups all-purpose flour

2 teaspoons baking powder

½ teaspoon baking soda

⅛ teaspoon cream of tartar

⅛ teaspoon salt

½ cup all natural peanut butter

½ cup unsalted butter

1 large egg

1 ripe medium banana, mashed

½ cup Splenda Brown Sugar Substitute

¼ cup Splenda

2 teaspoons vanilla

Directions

Preheat oven to 350°F.

Sift together the first five dry ingredients.

In a large mixer bowl, cream together the peanut butter and unsalted butter until fluffy. At low speed, mix in the egg, pureed banana, Splenda, and vanilla.

With the mixer at low speed, slowly add the sifted dry ingredients until fully mixed.

Shape dough into one-inch balls. Place on ungreased cookie sheet 1" (2.5cm) apart. Flatten cookies with the palm of your hand.

Bake for 12 – 14 minutes or until bottoms are golden brown.

Remove cookies from cookie sheets to wire rack, and cool completely.

Nutrition: 46 calories; 3g fat; 5g carbohydrates; 1g protein; per cookie

Pumpkin Cinnamon Cookies

Makes 14 cookies

Ingredients

3/4 cup Splenda Granular

1 cup rolled oats

1 cup whole wheat flour

1/2 cup soy flour

1 3/4 teaspoons baking soda

1/2 teaspoon baking powder

1/2 teaspoon salt

2 teaspoons ground cinnamon

1 teaspoon ground nutmeg

1/2 cup pumpkin puree

1 tablespoon canola oil

2 teaspoons water

2 egg whites

1 teaspoon molasses

1 tablespoon flax seeds (optional)

Directions

Preheat oven to 350 F.

In a large bowl, whisk together Splenda, oats, wheat flour, soy flour, baking soda, baking powder, salt, cinnamon, and nutmeg. Stir in pumpkin, canola oil, water, egg whites, and molasses. Stir in flax seeds, if desired. Roll into 14 large balls, and flatten on a baking sheet.

Bake for 5 minutes in preheated oven. Careful not to over bake or the cookies will be too dry.

Nutrition: 85 calories; 2g fat; 13g carbohydrates; 4g protein; per cookie

Almond Cookies
Makes 30 cookies

Ingredients

1 ½ cups almond flour

½ cup flax seed meal

¼ cup artificial sweetener

2 ounces walnuts, chopped

1 teaspoon baking powder

4 egg whites

1 ounce butter, softened

Directions

Preheat oven to 350°F. Combine and mix all dry ingredients.

Add softened butter and rub into dry ingredients until even and produces a slightly grainy texture. Add egg whites and mix well.

Using a leveled tablespoon, add dough onto parchment paper. Press each cookie down with a fork.

Bake 18-20 minutes. Remove and cool on a wire rack.

Nutrition: 31 calories; 3g fat; 1g carbohydrates; 1g protein; per cookie

Gingersnap Cookies
Makes 18 cookies

Ingredients

1 ⅓ cups whole spelt flour or 1 ⅓ cups whole wheat flour

¾ teaspoon baking soda

½ teaspoon ginger powder

¼ cup molasses

¼ cup brown sugar, keep a couple teaspoons aside for the top

3 tablespoons frozen orange juice concentrate, thawed

Directions

Preheat oven to 300F.

Mix ingredients all together in a bowl, roll into balls, press with a fork dipped into sugar. Place balls on baking sheet.

Bake at 300F about 12 minutes.

Nutrition: 30 calories; 0g fat; 7g carbohydrates; 0g protein; per cookie

Honey Raisin Cookies

Ingredients

½ cup butter, softened

½ cup honey

1 egg

1 teaspoon vanilla

1 cup whole wheat flour

1 teaspoon baking powder

¼ teaspoon salt

½ cup oats

½ cup raisins

½ cup chopped walnuts

Directions

Combine first 4 ingredients and mix well.

Combine next 4 ingredients and add to honey butter mixture. Add the raisins and chopped walnuts.

Bake at 350 degree F for 12-15 minutes or until just lightly golden brown.

Nutrition: 227 calories; 12g fat; 28g carbohydrates; 4g protein; per cookie

No-Bake Oatmeal Coconut Cookies
Makes 18 cookies

Ingredients

6 tablespoons sugar-free instant chocolate milk mix

1 teaspoon vanilla extract

½ cup margarine

½ cup 2% milk

1 cup flaked coconut

3 cups quick oatmeal

Directions

In food prosessor or mixer bowl add Sugar Free Quik, vanilla, margarine and milk and blend until smooth.

Add coconut and oatmeal and blend until mixed together well.

On a cookie sheet place a piece of wax paper and take spoonful of the mixture and roll into a ball place close together.

Refrigerate for 1 hour.

Nutrition: 92 calories; 6g fat; 9g carbohydrates; 1g
protein;   per   cookie

Peanut Butter Cookies

Ingredients

1 cup chunky natural peanut butter

¼ cup canola oil

½ cup packed dark brown sugar

½ cup granulated sugar

3 tablespoons low-fat plain yogurt

1 tablespoon vanilla extract

¾ cup all-purpose flour

2 large eggs

⅓ cup unsweetened cocoa powder

¼ cup rolled oats

1 teaspoon baking soda

½ teaspoon salt

¼ cup semisweet chocolate chips

¼ cup trans-fat-free peanut butter chips

¼ cup turbinado sugar

Directions

Preheat oven to 350°F.

Beat peanut butter, oil, brown sugar and granulated sugar in a large bowl with an electric mixer on medium speed until the sugars are blended. Beat in eggs, yogurt and vanilla until combined.

Whisk flour, cocoa, oats, baking soda and salt in a medium bowl. With the mixer on low speed, gradually add the dry ingredients to the peanut butter mixture until blended. It should be sticky. Stir in chocolate and peanut butter chips.

Using a small cookie scoop or slightly rounded tablespoons of dough, place cookies 2 inches apart on ungreased cookie sheets.

Dip the bottom of a glass in water and then in turbinado sugar. Use the sugared glass to flatten the cookies slightly, leaving a thin layer of sugar on top, rewetting the glass as needed.

Bake the cookies in batches until they are just set and the tops appear cracked, 8 to 10 minutes. Careful not to overbake cookies, or they will be too dry.

Cool on the baking sheet for 2 minutes before transferring to a wire rack to cool.

Nutrition: 117 calories; 6 g fat; 1 g fiber; 13 g carbohydrates; 3 g protein; per cookie

Banana Oat Cookies
Makes 12 cookies

Ingredients
2 ripe bananas, mashed

1/2 cup whole wheat flour

1/4 cup wheat bran

1/4 cup rolled oats

1/2 cup packed brown sugar

1/2 cup low-fat plain yogurt

1/8 cup real maple syrup

2 egg whites

1 teaspoon ground cinnamon

1/2 teaspoon salt

1/2 teaspoon baking powder

1/2 cup raisins

Directions
Preheat oven to 350F.

Beat mashed bannanas, egg whites, brown sugar, maple syrup, yogurt, and cinnamon.

Combine the remaining dry ingredients: flour, oats, wheat bran, salt and baking powder in a separate bowl. Use an electric mixer to combine dry ingredients with wet mixture.

Add in raisins.

Roll cookies into balls, place on a cookie sheet coated with cooking spray. Bake for 8-12 minutes until cookies are firm and dry.

Nutrition: 117 calories; 0.5g fat; 27g carbohydrates; 3g protein; per cookie

Banana Cookies
Makes 36 cookies

Ingredients

2 ¼ cups flour

1 teaspoon baking soda

1 teaspoon salt

¾ cup unsweetened applesauce

2 egg whites

½ cup Splenda sugar substitute

¼ cup sugar

½ cup Splenda brown sugar blend

1 medium banana, mashed

1 teaspoon vanilla

1 ¼ cups semi sweet chocolate chips

4 marshmallows, shredded

Directions
Preheat oven to 350°F.

Stir flour, salt and baking soda in a bowl, set aside. Beat applesauce, egg whites, and sugars with a mixer. Mix in bananas and vanilla.

Slowly add flour mixture to mixer. Add chocolate chips. Drop by spoonfuls onto cookie sheet.

Bake for 15 minutes.

Nutrition: 83 calories; 2g fat; 16g carbohydrates; 1g protein; per cookie

Raisin Oatmeal Cookies
Makes 24 cookies

Ingredients
1 cup self-rising flour

½ cup butter

2 tablespoons white Splenda granular

2 tablespoons milk

1 ½ cups quick oats

1 egg

¼ teaspoon cinnamon

⅓ cup Splenda brown sugar blend

½ teaspoon vanilla

½ cup dark raisins

Directions
Preheat the oven to 325 degrees.

In a bowl, mix the flour with the cinnamon.

In a separate bowl, cream the butter and both the sugars until fluffy. Add the egg, milk, and vanilla. Gradually add the flour mixture.

Stir in oats and raisins.

Drop by teaspoonfuls if small cookies are desired, or tablespoons if larger cookies are desired onto parchment paper.

Bake until golden brown, 10-12 minutes. Cool on wire racks.

Nutrition: 95 calories; 4.5g fat; 12g carbohydrates; 2g protein; per cookie

Chocolate Chip Cookies

Ingredients

1-1/2 cups whole wheat flour

1/2 cups old-fashioned or quick oats

1 teaspoon baking soda

1 teaspoon cinnamon

1/8 teaspoon nutmeg

1/8 teaspoon cloves

1/2 teaspoon salt

3/4 cup butter

3 Tablespoons vegetable oil

1/3 cup Stevia Extract in the Raw

1/4 cup brown sugar

2 eggs

2 teaspoons vanilla extract

3/4 cup Sugar Free Chocolate Chips

1/4 cup walnuts, chopped

Directions

Preheat oven to 375F. Beat butter and oil, Splenda, sugar, and vanilla in large bowl until creamy. Add eggs and beat well. Add dry ingredients, mixing until combined.

Stir in chocolate chips and nuts. Drop by rounded teaspoon onto ungreased cookie sheet. You should have enough dough to make 4 dozen cookies.

Bake 7-9 minutes or until edges are lightly browned; Cool slightly; remove to wire rack to cool.

Nutrition: 118 calories; 8 g fat; 1 g fiber; 10 g carbohydrates; 1 g protein; per cookie

Cheesecake Brownies

Ingredients

Cheesecake Topping

4 ounces reduced-fat cream cheese

¼ cup sugar

1 large egg

1 tablespoon all-purpose flour

1 tablespoon nonfat plain yogurt

½ teaspoon vanilla extract

Brownie

⅔ cup whole-wheat pastry flour

½ cup unsweetened cocoa powder

¼ teaspoon salt

1 large egg

2 large egg whites, or 4 teaspoons dried egg, prepared according to package directions

1¼ cups packed light brown sugar

¼ cup canola oil

¼ cup strong coffee, or black tea

2 teaspoons vanilla extract

Directions

Preheat oven to 350°F. Coat a 7-by-11-inch brownie pan or baking pan with cooking spray.

To prepare topping: Place cream cheese in a small mixing bowl and beat with an electric mixer until smooth and creamy. Add sugar and beat until smooth. Add egg, flour, yogurt and vanilla; beat until well blended.

To prepare brownie layer: Whisk whole-wheat flour, cocoa and salt in a bowl. Place egg, egg whites and brown sugar in a large bowl and beat with the electric mixer on medium speed until smooth. Add oil, coffee or tea and vanilla; beat until well blended. Add the dry ingredients and beat on low speed just until well blended, stopping once to scrape down the sides.

Scrape about half of the brownie batter into the prepared pan. Slowly pour the topping evenly on top. Drop the remaining brownie batter in large dollops over the topping. Draw the tip of a sharp knife or skewer through the two batters to create a swirled effect.

Bake the brownies until the top is just firm to the touch, about 20 minutes. Let cool completely in the pan on a wire rack. Coat a knife with cooking spray and cut into 24 bars.

Nutrition: 100 calories; 4 g fat; 16 g carbohydrates; 2 g protein; per 1/24 of recipe

Banana Oatmeal Raisin Cookies

Makes 24 cookies

Ingredients

3 bananas, mashed

2 cups quick-cooking oats

⅓ cup applesauce

¼ cup skim milk

¼ cup raisins (optional)

1 teaspoon vanilla extract

Directions

Combine all ingredients, beating well. Let stand 5 minutes so oats will absorb moisture.

Drop dough by heaping teaspoonfuls onto ungreased cookie sheets.

Bake at 350 degrees for 15-20 minutes. Let stand 1 minute on cookie sheets.

Transfer to wire racks and cool.

Nutrition: 43 calories; 0.5g fat; 9g carbohydrates; 1g protein; per cookie

Butterscotch Cookies
Makes 48 cookies

Ingredients

½ cup margarine, low sat fat (or butter, softened)

1 cup Splenda sugar substitute

½ cup packed Splenda sugar substitute, brown blend

1 teaspoon baking powder

½ teaspoon baking soda

½ teaspoon salt

½ cup egg white

2 teaspoons vanilla

2 cups white whole wheat flour

¾ cup coarsely chopped salted roasted cashews

⅔ cup butterscotch chips

Directions

Preheat oven to 375 degrees F.

In a large bowl, beat margarine or butter with an electric mixer on medium to high speed for 30 seconds. Add Splenda, baking powder, baking soda, and salt.

Beat until combined, scraping side of bowl occasionally.

Add egg whites and vanilla; beat until combined. Beat in as much of the flour as you can with the mixer. Using a wooden spoon, stir in any remaining flour. Stir in cashews and butterscotch chips.

Drop dough by rounded teaspoons 2 inches apart onto an ungreased cookie sheet.

Bake in preheated oven for 8 to 10 minutes or until edges are lightly browned. Transfer cookies to a wire rack; let cool.

Nutrition: 58 calories; 3g fat; 7 g carbohydrates; 1 g protein; per cookie

No Bake Oatmeal Peanut Butter Cookies

Makes 30 cookies

Ingredients

½ cup light margarine

½ cup skim milk

2 cups Splenda sugar substitute

3 tablespoons cocoa

½ cup reduced-fat peanut butter

1 teaspoon vanilla

3 cups quick-cooking oats

Directions

Bring margarine, milk, Splenda, and cocoa to a boil in medium saucepan. Boil for 1 minute.

Remove from heat. Stir in peanut butter and vanilla until combined.

Stir in oats. Drop by spoonfuls on wax paper or parchment paper.

61

Allow to cool completely before eating.

Nutrition: 47 calories; 1g fat; 9g carbohydrates; 1g protein; per cookie

Made in the USA
Middletown, DE
22 February 2018